Kids Can Draw
THE OCEAN

by Philippe Legendre

Walter Foster

Attention Parents and Teachers

All children can draw a circle, a square, or a triangle…which means that they can also learn to draw a dolphin, crab, or sailboat! The KIDS CAN DRAW learning method is easy and fun. Children will learn a technique and a vocabulary of shapes that will form the basis for all kinds of drawing.

Pictures are created by combining geometric shapes to form a mass of volumes and surfaces. From this stage, children can give character to their sketches with straight, curved, or broken lines.

With just a few strokes of the pencil, an ocean scene will appear—and with the addition of color, the picture will be real work of art!

The KIDS CAN DRAW method offers a real apprenticeship in technique and a first look at composition, proportion, shapes, and lines. The simplicity of this method ensures that the pleasure of drawing is always the most important factor.

About Philippe Legendre

French painter, engraver, and illustrator, Philippe Legendre also runs a school of art for children aged 6–14 years. Legendre frequently spends time in schools and has developed this method of learning so that all children can discover the artist within themselves.

Helpful Tips

1. Each picture is made up of simple geometric shapes, which are illustrated at the top of the left-hand page. This is called the **Vocabulary of Shapes.** Encourage children to practice drawing each shape before starting their pictures.

2. Suggest children use a pencil to do their sketches. This way, if they don't like a particular shape, they can just erase it and try again.

3. A dotted line indicates that the line should be erased. Have children draw the whole shape and then erase the dotted part of the line.

4. Once children finish their drawings, they can color them with crayons, colored pencils, or felt-tip markers. They may want to go over the lines with a black pencil or pen.

Now let's get started!

With five red legs,

he's really not a fish.

Just find his star shape,

close your eyes, and make a wish.

Starfish

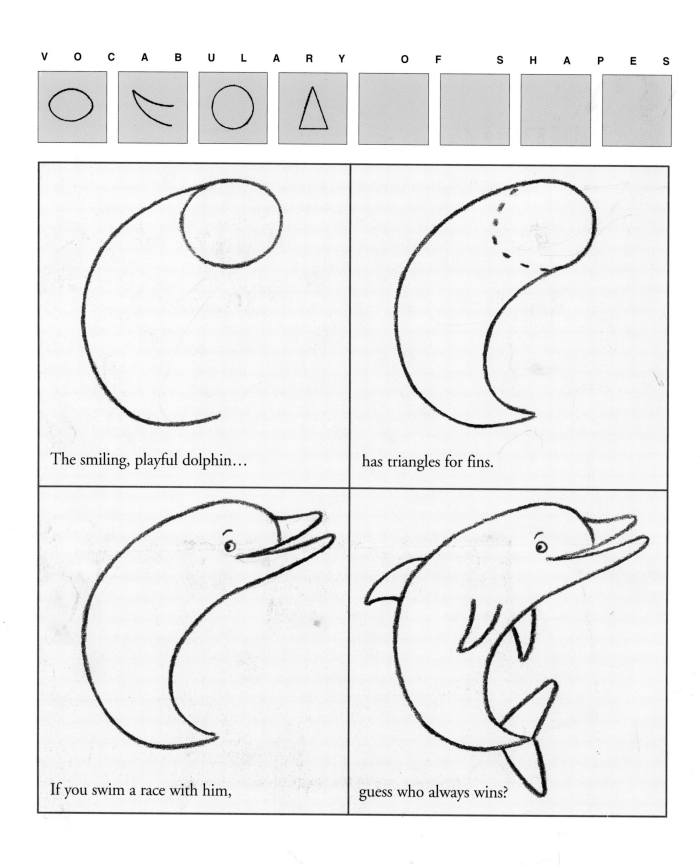

The smiling, playful dolphin…

has triangles for fins.

If you swim a race with him,

guess who always wins?

Dolphin

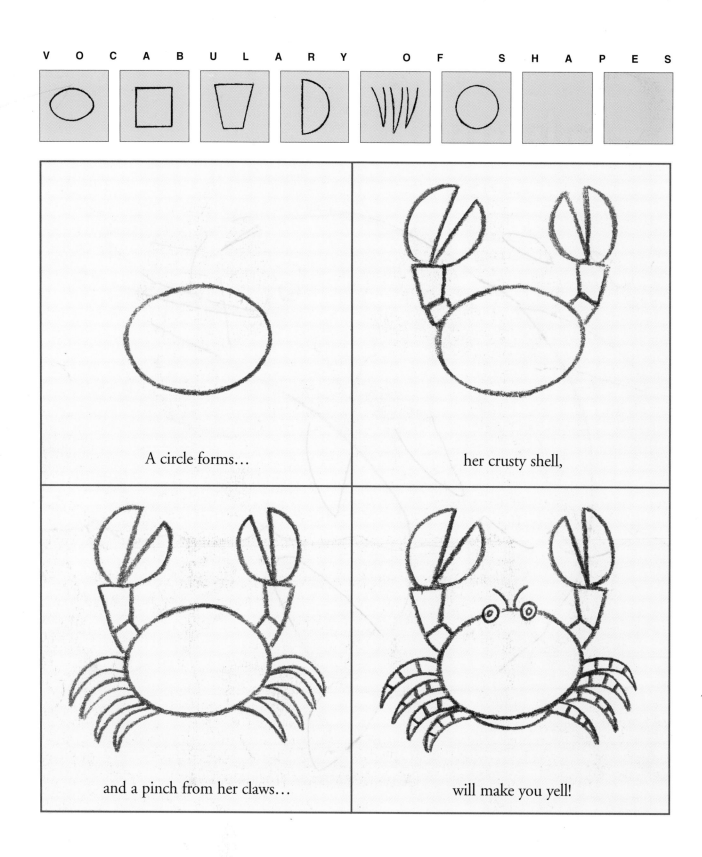

A circle forms…

her crusty shell,

and a pinch from her claws…

will make you yell!

Crab

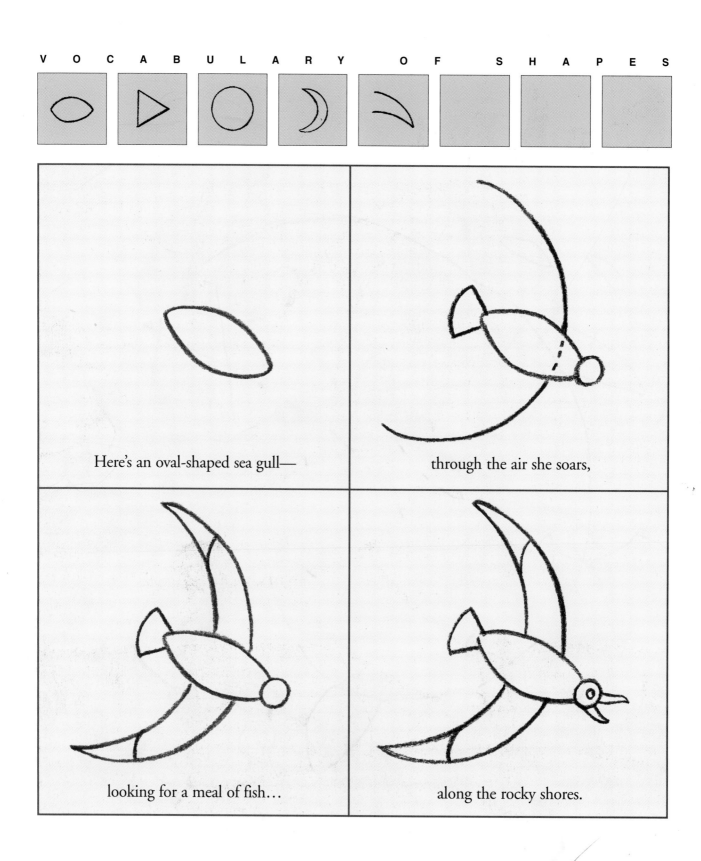

Here's an oval-shaped sea gull—

through the air she soars,

looking for a meal of fish…

along the rocky shores.

Sea Gull

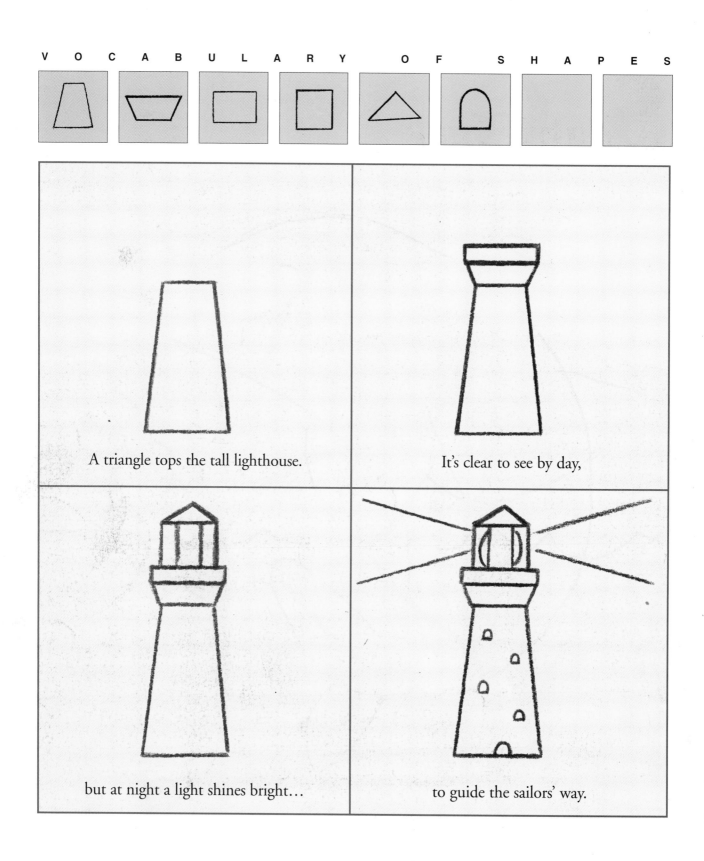

A triangle tops the tall lighthouse.

It's clear to see by day,

but at night a light shines bright...

to guide the sailors' way.

Lighthouse

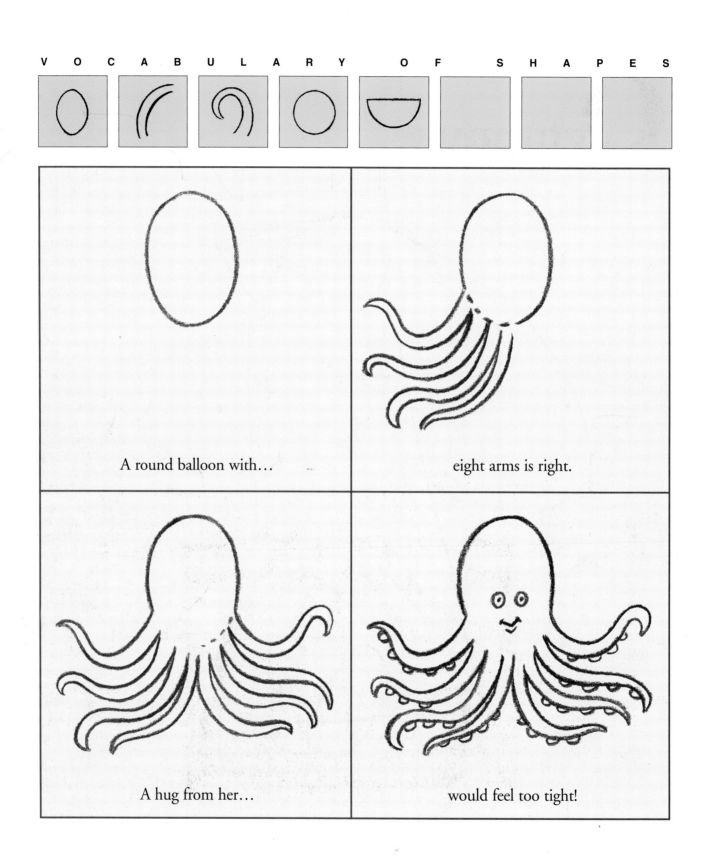

A round balloon with…

eight arms is right.

A hug from her…

would feel too tight!

Octopus

A triangle…

is all he needs…

to help him sail…

the seven seas.

Windsurfer

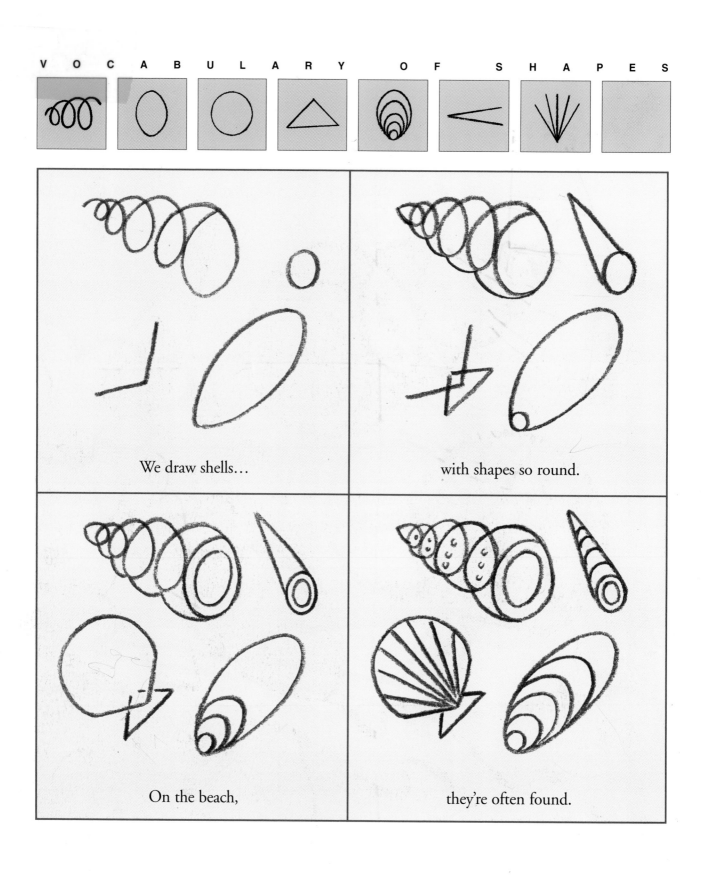

We draw shells…

with shapes so round.

On the beach,

they're often found.

Shells

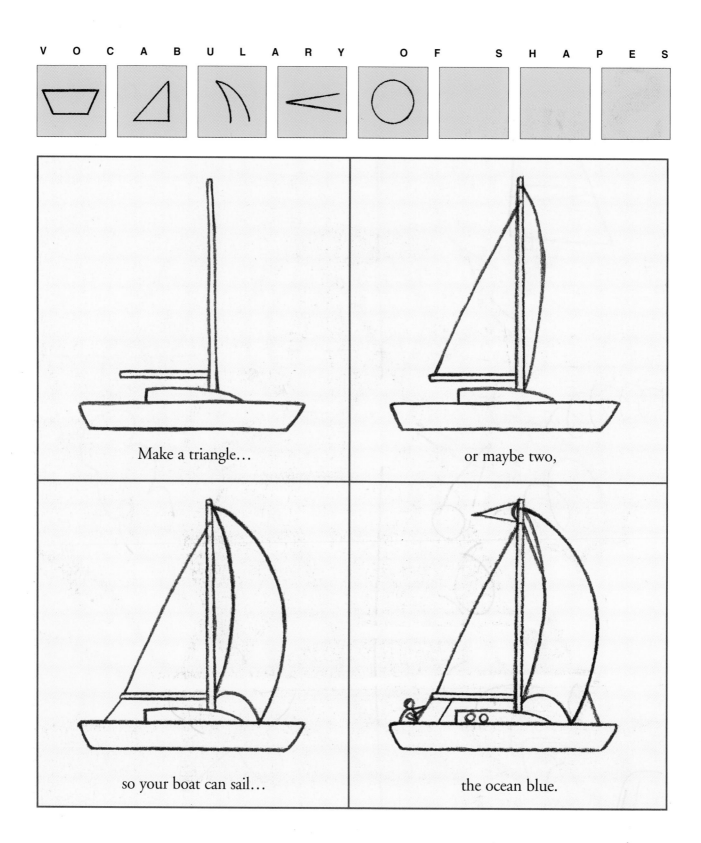

Make a triangle…

or maybe two,

so your boat can sail…

the ocean blue.

Sailboat

Now that you have practiced and can draw them all with ease,

you can make a picture of the life around the seas.

Draw-along fun for children!

With the "I Can Draw" series, kids ages 6 and up will have hours of fun drawing amazing pictures of the things they like best—animals, cartoons, creepy creatures, race cars, and more. Each book is full of colorful step-by-step illustrations with easy-to-follow instructions. Kids will learn how to draw almost anything by starting with the basic shapes they already know, such as circles, squares, triangles, and ovals. Each 40-page book includes 8 pages of grid paper.

Walter Foster

For a free catalog, write to Walter Foster Publishing, Inc.
23062 La Cadena Drive, Laguna Hills, CA 92653
800/426-0099 • www.walterfoster.com